LANDF🌍RMS

CONTINENTS

Sandy Sepehri

Rourke
Publishing LLC
Vero Beach, Florida 32964

www.rourkepublishing.com

Photo Credits

Pg. 5 © Wikimedia Commons; Pg. 6 © Steffen Foerster Photography; Pg. 7 © USGS; Pg. 10 © Vova Pomortzeff; Pg. 11 © Franck Camhi; Pg. 11b © Antonio Jorge Nunes; Pg. 11c Svetlana Privezentseva; Pg. 12 © Dvoretskiy Igor Vladimirovich; Pg. 12b © Marco Alegria; Pg. 13 © Hannes Grobe; Pg. 14 © National Science Foundation; Pg. 14b © National Science Foundation; Pg. 15 © National Science Foundation; Pg. 15b © Jose Alberto Tejo; Pg. 16 © Efremova Irina; Pg. 19 © Ronald Sumners; Pg. 20 © Steve Lovegrove; Pg. 21 © Susan Flashman; Pg. 21b © Eric Isselée; Pg. 21c © Susan Flashman; Pg. 22 © Svetlana Privezentseva; Pg. 23 © gary718; Pg. 23b © Alexey Goosev; Pg. 26 © Mike Norton; Pg. 27 © Teck Siong Ong; Pg. 27b © Wikipedia; Pg. 28 © Socrates; Pg. 30 © Ranplett.

Design and Production - Blue Door Publishing; bdpublishing.com

Library of Congress Cataloging-in-Publication Data

Sepehri, Sandy.
 Continents / Sandy Sepehri.
   p. cm. -- (Landforms)
  ISBN 978-1-60044-548-4 (hard cover)
  ISBN 978-1-60694-910-8 (soft cover)
1. Continents--Juvenile literature. I. Title.
G133.S47 2008
910.914'1--dc22

                                    2007012141

Rourke Publishing
Printed in the United States of America, North Mankato, Minnesota
083110
082710LP-A

ROURKE
PUBLISHING
www.rourkepublishing.com - rourke@rourkepublishing.com
Post Office Box 643328 Vero Beach, Florida 32964

Table of Contents

The Big Blue Marble

When seen from space, the Earth looks just like a big blue marble. Its swirling patterns of white are actually clouds, and its warm-colored areas of green and brown are masses of land, known as the seven **continents**.

Unlike a marble, the Earth is always changing. You may feel perfectly still, but you are on a continent that is slowly drifting in the ocean.

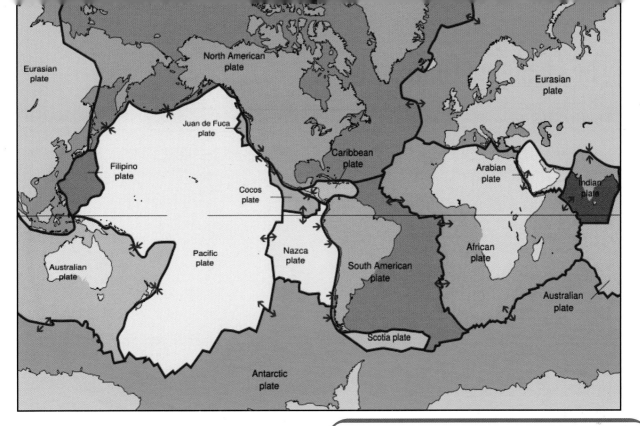

The surface of the Earth is not a solid skin, like on a piece of fruit. It is divided into separate areas, called plates, which lie under the continents and oceans.

The plates are composed of the Earth's crust and rocks from the mantle layer, and they move only a few centimeters a year. What's making them move is called **plate tectonics**.

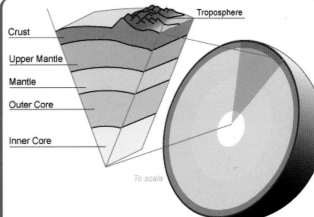

Have you ever examined a loaf of fresh bread? It's warm and moist on the inside and hard and crunchy on the outside. Likewise, the Earth is covered with a crust, and underneath lie layers where it's so hot that rocks melt!

The Changing Continents

Pangaea the Supercontinent

The Earth's plates are always moving, and with them move the continents. This is called continental drift. If you cut out paper pictures of the continents, you could fit them back together in one big piece. This is roughly what the continents looked like 248 million years ago. This supercontinent is named *Pangaea*, a Greek word, which means "all the Earth."

Pangaea was home to the first dinosaurs and mammals that appeared on Earth during the Triassic period. New dinosaurs continued to appear, up until the end of the Cretaceous period, 65 million years ago.

Laurasia and Gondwana

By the beginning of the Jurassic Period, 206 million years ago, Pangaea split into two distinct landmasses: Laurasia and Gondwana. Laurasia contained what are now North America, Europe, and part of Asia. Gondwana contained what are now Antarctica, South America, Africa, Madagascar, Australia, New Guinea, New Zealand, Arabia, and India.

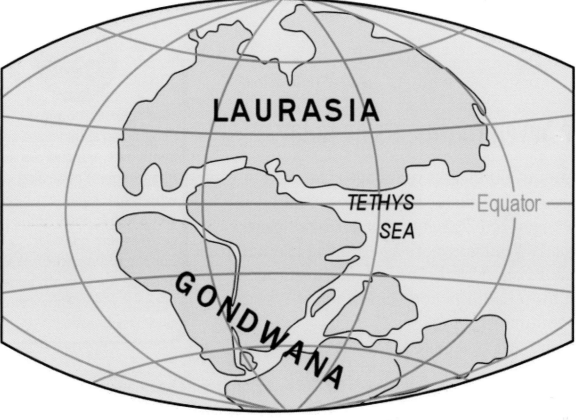

A SUPERCONTINENT SPLITS

It is believed that the supercontinent made its final split around 200 million years ago during the end of the Triassic period.

North America

Europe

Asia

Africa

South America

Australia

Antarctica

The Seven Continents of Today

About 200 million years ago, Laurasia began to break into smaller landmasses. Gondwana also began to break into smaller landmasses, about 167 million years ago, during the mid-to-late Jurassic Period. These broken off pieces of land from Laurasia and Gondwana are what we call continents.

From largest to smallest, they are:

According to most geographers, there are seven continents, but there is some disagreement regarding where one continent begins and another ends. Some geographers consider Europe to be part of Asia because the two are joined in some areas. They call this landmass Eurasia.

Asia	16,910,884 sq. mi.	43,810,582 sq. km.
Africa	11,668,545 sq. mi.	30,221,532 sq. km.
North America	9,450,000 sq. mi.	24,490,000 sq. km.
South America	6,890,000 sq. mi.	17,840,000 sq. km.
Europe	3,930,000 sq. mi.	10,180,000 sq. km.
Antarctica	5,405,430 sq. mi.	14,400,000 sq. km.
Australia	3,304160 sq. mi.	8,560,000 sq. km.

The continents are still moving today. In the middle of the Atlantic Ocean floor, between two Earth plates, is a deep crack called the Mid-Atlantic Ridge. These plates are constantly, but slowly, pulling away from each other, putting more and more distance between them. As the plates move away from each other, so do the continents on top of them.

Geologists believe that North America will eventually drift so far west it will reach Asia. They also expect California to break off from North America and float away.

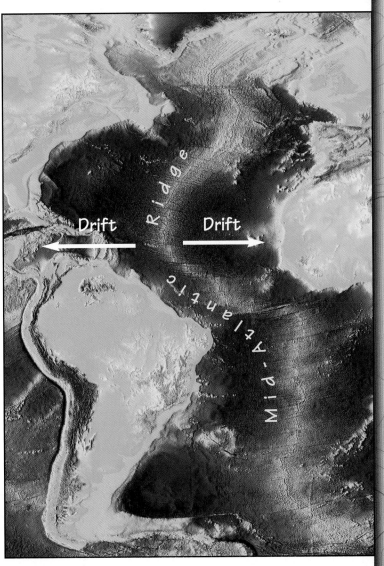

This map shows the Mid-Atlantic Ridge running nearly pole to pole across the Earth. This break between two plates is thousands of miles long.

How does the ocean floor grow?

When the Earth's plates pull apart and tear an opening in the crust, the underlying hot magma flows up to fill the space. The magma dries and hardens into new crust.

First Stop: Africa

The second largest continent on Earth is Africa. It holds more than 50 countries.

North Africa is mostly dry and features Mount Kilimanjaro and the Sahara Desert, the largest desert in the world. Central Africa is crossed by the equator, where warm rain forests are home to many rare animals such as forest elephants and leopards. Southern Africa has mines that provide a major source of the world's 12 main **mineral** resources.

Africa

Equator

Mount Kilimanjaro is the highest mountain in Africa, 19,340 feet (95,895 m).

Lake Victoria is the largest lake in Africa, and the second largest freshwater lake in the world. (Lake Superior in North America is the largest freshwater lake).

Africa's diverse landscape includes dry deserts and lush, tropical rain forests.

The Nile is the longest river in the world. It flows north through East Africa, Egypt, and into the Mediterranean Sea. It brings water and fertile soil to its surrounding areas.

Africa has the second highest population in the world, including hundreds of different ethnic groups. More than two thousand languages are spoken here, and many Africans speak more than one.

The Massai are one of many ethnic groups living in Africa. They live in Kenya and northern Tanzania.

Most of the people in North Africa are Arabs or Berbers. Bedouins, like the man above, are an ethnic group living in North Africa.

The most fertile area in Africa is the Congo Basin, receiving more than 60 inches (152 cm) of rain a year.

Africa produces many of the world's minerals and the majority of diamonds and gold. Africa processes agricultural crops, fish and fruits, and manufactures building materials and textiles.

Tutankhamun's mummy was buried with a gold mask. Today, Africa is still rich in gold.

Egypt is in North Africa. Egypt is home to the great pyramids, and where the tomb of Tutankhamun was found.

Africa is also known for its devastating periods of drought. A drought occurs when there is not enough water to support the needs of people, animals, and plants. Even during times of average rainfall, drought can occur from a lack of groundwater supply or even from the type of agricultural techniques used.

Dirt and dust replaces grasslands and crops in a drought.

Antarctica

Antarctica is the world's coldest continent. It is almost completely covered by an ice sheet that has been building up for millions of years. At the coast, pieces of it break off and become icebergs. Dividing the ice sheet into two sections are the Transantarctic Mountains, which extend across the continent. On one side of the mountains, the ice sheet is mostly above sea level. On the other side, it is mostly below sea level.

GEOGRAPHIC AREA: The Ross Ice Shelf is bigger than France and is an average of 1,000 feet (300 m) thick.

The Transantarctic Mountains is one of the longest mountain ranges on Earth and has a length of 2,175 miles (3,500 km).

The Transantarctic Mountains.

13

The U.S. Coast Guard icebreaker approaches the Ross Ice Shelf.

Scientists work on a weather monitoring device.

The only human residents of Antarctica are scientists, mostly there for the summer. These scientists have brought back valuable information about this continent's animals and weather.

Some of the first people to go to Antarctica were whalers and sealers. In 1778, they started hunting seals for their oil and fur, until they almost became **extinct**. Since 1978, seal hunting has been limited. In the early 1900s, Antarctic whales were also hunted almost to extinction, but have since become protected.

Beware the Meltdown!
If global warming continues, scientists predict that Antarctica's western ice sheet could melt, possibly as soon as the next hundred years. This meltdown of ice could raise the world's sea level by 20 feet (6 m).

On land, there is very little life in Antarctica and only a few plants and insects. However, the surrounding ocean is full of marine life and the sea animals which need them for food, including seals, penguins, and whales.

The Antarctic is home to the rarely seen ross seal, the huge elephant seal and the leopard seal, which eats penguins. Penguins catch their food underwater and climb on board the land to breed and care for their eggs.

Emperor Penguin.

The leopard seal is the second largest seal in Antarctica and can live up to 26 years.

Asia

Asia is the largest continent on Earth, with 49 countries. It has almost every type of landscape, including the Tibetan-Qinghai Highlands in China—the highest and largest **plateau** in the world, and the Himalayas—the highest mountain range in the world.

On the great plain of Siberia, in Russia, winters are bitterly cold and the sun shines for only an hour a day. In southern Asia, in India, the weather is mostly hot and can reach 120°F (48°C).

Mount Everest is the highest mountain on Earth. It is 29,028 feet (8,848 m). It is part of the Himalaya range on the border between Nepal and China.

In southern Asia, the weather is hot and can make working outside very difficult.

Monsoons
Monsoons occur mostly in Asia. Monsoon winds bring heavy rain in the summer that can last for months. In the winter, the winds bring dry air.

Iran, Iraq, and the countries on the Arabian peninsula are part of a region called the Middle East. In Central Asia, the Middle East has one the largest oil reserves in the world.

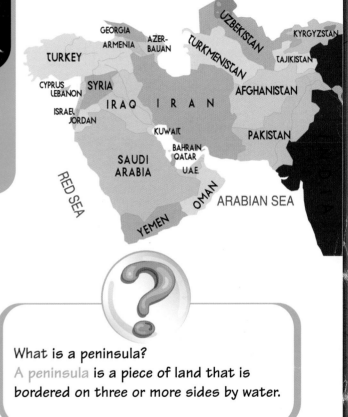

Aden, Yemen, has less than two inches of rain per year.
Mawsynram, India, gets 467 inches (1,186 cm) of rain a year.

What is a peninsula?
A peninsula is a piece of land that is bordered on three or more sides by water.

The Asian brown cloud is what scientists call the thick blanket of pollution that hangs over South and Southeast Asia. It is two miles (three kilometers) thick and is caused by people burning fuels. It is so severe that it could create dangerous weather patterns, and cause millions of people to become very sick.

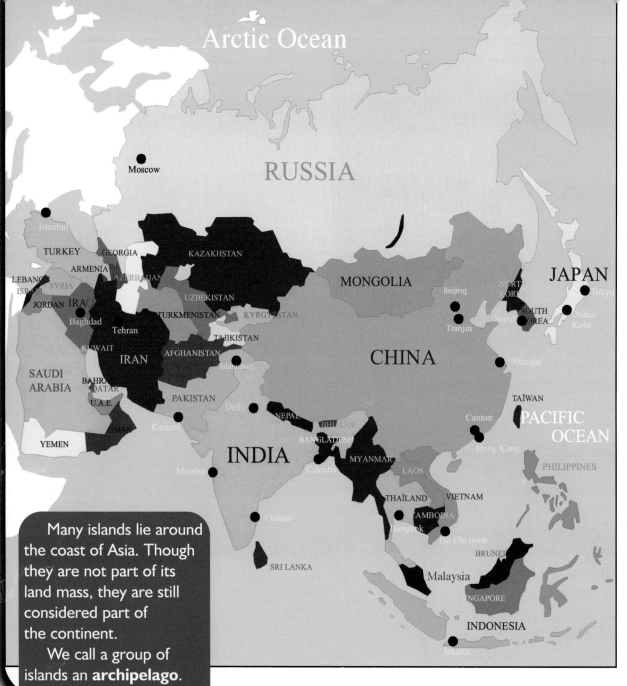

Arctic Ocean

RUSSIA

Moscow

Istanbul

TURKEY

GEORGIA

ARMENIA

LEBANON

ISRAEL

SYRIA

AZERBAIJAN

JORDAN

IRAQ

Baghdad

KUWAIT

Tehran

SAUDI
ARABIA

BAHRAIN

QATAR

U.A.E.

IRAN

OMAN

YEMEN

KAZAKHSTAN

UZBEKISTAN

TURKMENISTAN

KYRGYZSTAN

TAJIKISTAN

AFGHANISTAN

Islamabad

PAKISTAN

Karachi

MONGOLIA

Beijing

Tianjin

CHINA

Delhi

NEPAL

BHUTAN

BANGLADESH

INDIA

Mumbai

Calcutta

MYANMAR

LAOS

Chennai

THAILAND

VIETNAM

Bangkok

CAMBODIA

SRI LANKA

Ho Chi minh

Malaysia

SINGAPORE

INDONESIA

Jakarta

JAPAN

Tokyo

NORTH
KOREA

Seoul

SOUTH
KOREA

Osaka/
Kobe

Shangai

TAIWAN

Canton

Hong Kong

PACIFIC
OCEAN

PHILIPPINES

BRUNEI

Many islands lie around
the coast of Asia. Though
they are not part of its
land mass, they are still
considered part of
the continent.

We call a group of
islands an **archipelago**.
Japan is an archipelago. It
is a group of islands off
the east coast of Asia in
the Pacific Ocean.

Within Asia the continent are subcontinents.
Subcontinents are large areas of land that are
part of a continent but considered separate
because of their geography or politics. India is
a subcontinent.

Australia

Australia, 'the land down under,' is entirely in the Southern **Hemisphere**, meaning below the equator. It is also the smallest continent, as well as the flattest and most **arid**. To its south are the cold waters of the Antarctic Ocean; and to its north are warm **tropical** seas beneath Southeast Asia. Two thirds of Australia is desert or semi-desert.

Continent or Country?
Australia is the only continent that is both a continent and a country. The islands, Tasmania and Melville, are separate from the continent of Australia, but considered part of the country.

Because Australia is in the Southern Hemisphere, the seasons are the opposite to the seasons in North America. When we are having winter, they are having summer!

Uluru, or Ayers Rock, is a giant sandstone rock located in the center of Australia. The rock attracts millions of tourists every year.

Most of Australia has the oldest and least **fertile** soil in the world, though along the east coast is fertile farmland.

Farmers in Australia grow wheat, cotton, bananas, cocoa, and sugarcane. Some people run sheep stations, raising sheep for their wool and meat. Most sheep stations in Australia are in the outback. *Outback* mostly

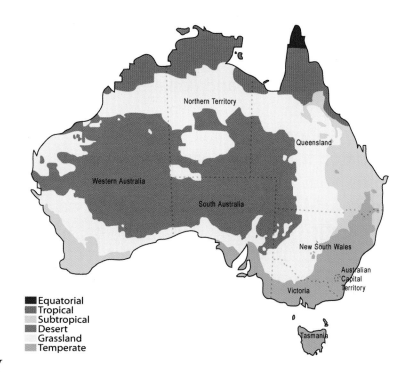

refers to remote and arid areas of Australia. The outback is extremely rich in iron, aluminum, manganese and uranium ores, and also contains major deposits of gold, nickel, lead, and zinc ores.

The landscapes of the northern part of the country, with a tropical climate, consist of rainforest, woodland, grassland, mangrove swamps, and desert.

In Australia, sheep stations are usually in the outback.

Australia's Great Barrier Reef is located off the northeastern coast. It is the world's largest coral reef and is so big it can be seen from space!

Tasmania is an island located 125 miles (200 km) south of the eastern side of the continent, being separated from it by Bass **Strait**. The state of Tasmania includes the island of Tasmania, and other surrounding islands. It is part of the continent of Australia.

Some of Australia's animals are found nowhere else on Earth, including koalas, wombats, kangaroos, and wallabies—all marsupials, meaning they carry their babies in an abdominal pouch.

Europe

Europe is the second smallest continent, with 40 independent countries. It is actually a peninsula of the much larger landmass Eurasia.

Northern Europe's landforms include snow-capped mountains, waterfalls, volcanoes, and hot springs. Southern Europe, along the warm Mediterranean Sea, has olive groves and vineyards. Eastern Europe is separated from Russia by the Ural Mountains, where there is oil, coal, iron, copper, gold, and gemstones.

Eurasia is a land mass which includes the continents of Europe and Asia.

View of Geirangerfjord in Norway, Europe.

View of the Mediterranean Sea from Tarragona, Spain.

Europe is a peninsula—it is surrounded by water on three sides. It breaks into smaller peninsulas all around its coast.

A view of the Alps from a ski resort in Switzerland.

Out of all the mountain ranges stretching across Europe, the Alps are the highest. They lie across nine countries and are the source of many major European rivers.

Europe has many regions. Each region may have the same weather, landforms, or culture. Scandinavia is a region, it is made up of Denmark, Sweden, Norway, Finland, and Iceland.

In mid-summer, northern Scandinavia has sunlight 24 hours a day!

Russia

Russia actually crosses two continents: Asia and Europe. Russia is divided by the Ural Mountains. The Ural Mountains separate eastern Russia and the rest of Europe from Asia.

Europe is home to many ethnic groups and 40 major languages. Its economy is largely based upon industry and services, as well as farming. Worldwide fishing industries are in Russia, Poland, and Germany. Eastern Europe grows corn and spring wheat, while Southern Europe specializes in fruits and vegetables.

Europe is plentiful in coal, iron ore, and manganese, an **alloy** that hardens steel.

North America

North America lies in the Northern Hemisphere. It includes the United States, Canada, Central America, the island of Greenland, and all of the countries of the Caribbean. It is the third largest continent.

It includes 23 countries and dozens of possessions and **territories**, located mostly in the Caribbean. To the north, Alaska, Canada, and Greenland touch the icy Arctic Ocean. North America is bordered on the east by the North Atlantic Ocean, on the southeast by the Caribbean Sea, and on the south and west by the North Pacific Ocean. It is connected to South America, by the Isthmus of Panama.

MAJOR REGIONS OF NORTH AMERICA

Major Region:	Features:
Western Region	Rocky Mountains and the Great Basin (a large, arid region of the Western United States)
Eastern Region	Appalachian Mountains
Northeastern Region	The Canadian Shield (a plateau)
The Great Plains	Gulf of Mexico and the Canadian Arctic

What is an isthmus?
An isthmus is a narrow strip of land (with water on both sides) connecting two larger land areas.

The United States

The Eastern United States, has mostly **deciduous** vegetation and grasslands. Prairies, boreal forests, and the Rocky Mountains are in the west, and deserts in the southwest. Because of its large size and many different geographic features there are many different climates. Southern Florida is tropical, Alaska is **polar**. (Alaska is separated from the United States by Canada). The states bordering the Gulf of Mexico are prone to hurricanes and most of the world's tornadoes occur within the continental United States.

Old Faithful Geyser is one of the most popular features in Yellowstone.

There are many National Parks throughout the United States. Yellowstone became the world's first national park on March 1, 1872. Located mostly in the U.S. state of Wyoming, the park extends into Montana and Idaho. The park is known for its **geothermal** features.

The Grand Canyon is a very colorful, steep-sided gorge, carved by the Colorado River, in Arizona. In some places the canyon is over a mile (1.6 km) deep. The canyon is the result of about 6 million years of erosion.

Everglades

The Florida Everglades are subtropical marshland located in the southern portion of the U.S. state of Florida.

California, on the west coast, is home to the giant Sequoia trees. These are thought to be the tallest trees in the world. Some of them are about 2,000 years old. They can grow to 379 feet (115.5 m) in height and 23 feet (7 m) diameter at the base.

The Everglades National Park in Florida covers 2.3 million acres. Water from the Everglades is used as a water supply for major cities in the area.

Where is the lowest point in North America?
Death Valley is the location of the lowest elevation in North America at 282 feet (86 m) below sea level.

Canada

Canada shares its borders with the United States. It has the world's longest coastline of 125,567 miles (202,080 km). Travel around Canada and you will see icy arctic regions, boreal forest, rocky mountains, flat prairies, and sparkling lakes.

A vast rock base known as the Canadian Shield

Canada holds vast reserves of water: its rivers discharge nearly nine percent of the world's renewable water supply, it contains a quarter of the world's wetlands, and it has the third largest amount of glaciers (after Antarctica and Greenland).

stretches north from the Great Lakes to the Arctic Ocean, covering half the country.

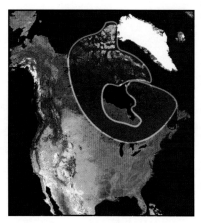

The Canadian Shield, shown as the blue area on the map.

The Caribbean

The Caribbean is an area in the southern portion of North America. This area is made up of nearly 7,000 islands, inlets, and cays. The area is surrounded by the warm and clear Caribbean Sea. The island terrain varies from flat and sandy to mountainous and rocky. The sea life is some of the most diverse in the world and millions of people visit this region every year for the beaches and water recreation.

South America

Equator

Most of South America is south of the equator. It is bordered on the west by the Pacific Ocean and on the north and east by the Atlantic Ocean. Its regions include the Andean States, the Guianas, the Southern Cone and Brazil, which is its largest and most populated country. Its natural resources are copper, iron ore, tin, and oil. It mainly produces coffee, sugarcane, and cotton.

One of the most famous landmarks in South America is the southern tip of land called Cape Horn. Ships passing this extreme, southern portion of land are confronted by violent storms and some of the roughest seas on Earth. For ships transporting cargo from the Atlantic Ocean to the Pacific Ocean, this was the only route until 1914 when the Panama Canal was built on the southern end of North America.

The barren land of Cape Horn.

South America

Atlantic Ocean

Cape Horn

South America has many of the world's most impressive landforms:

Angel Falls:	**Highest waterfall — 3,212 feet (979 m)** **Location: Canaima National Park, Venezuela**
Amazon River:	**Largest river (by volume) — about 4,000 miles (6,400 km) in length**
The Andes:	**Longest mountain range — 4,400 miles (7,000 km) long**
Atacama:	**Driest desert. Location: Chile**
Amazon Rainforest:	**Largest rainforest — (2.2 million square miles (5.5 million square km)**
Lake Titicaca:	**Highest commercially navigable lake — 12,507 feet (3,812 m) above sea level.** **Location: In the Andes on the border of Peru and Bolivia**

The Amazonian rainforest is home to millions of insects, tens of thousands of plants, and some 2000 birds and mammals. Deforestation, the cutting down of trees, is threatening the rainforest and its inhabitants.

Deforestation in the Amazon Rainforest threatens many species, including tree frogs.

The Amazon rainforest makes up over half of the Earth's remaining rainforests.

Glossary

archipelago (ar kuh PEL uh goh) — a group of islands

alloy (AL oi) — when two or more metals are mixed together

arid (A rid) — an area of land that is dry and receives little or no rainfall

continents (KON tuh nuhnts) — the seven large land masses on Earth

deciduous (di SIJ oo uhss) — deciduous trees lose their leaves every year

extinct (ek STINGKT) — a animal or plant species that no longer lives on Earth

fertile (FUR tuhl) — fertile land is good for growing plants and crops

geologist (jee OL uh jest) — a person who studies Earth's soil and rocks

geothermal (jee oh THUR muhl) — thermal energy or heat contained within the rocks below the Earth's surface

hemisphere (HEM uhss fihr) — one half of a sphere; one half of the Earth or the Northern Hemisphere and Southern Hemisphere

mineral (MIN ur uhl) — a substance on Earth; gold, copper, salt, silver

plate tectonics (PLAYT tek TON eeks) — the motion of large land masses that make up the Earth's crust

plateau (pla TOH) — an area of high flat land

polar (POH lur) — to do with the area around Earth's North and South Poles

strait (STRAYT) — a narrow strip of water connecting two larger bodies of water

territories (TER uh tor eez) — a large area of land often controlled by a person or government

tropical (TROP uh kuhl) — to do with the hot rainy area near the equator around the Earth

Index

Further Reading

Mara, Wil. *The Seven Continents*. Scholastic, 2005.
McClish, Bruce. *Earth's Continents*. Heinemann, 2003.
Bingham, Jane. *Europe*. Heinemann, 2007.

Websites To Visit

www.kids.earth.nasa.gov/archive/pangaea/
www.enchantedlearning.com/geography/continents/

About the Author

Sandy Sepehri lives with her husband, Shahram, and their three children in Florida. She has a bachelor's degree and writes freelance articles and children's stories. She has also written a number of fiction and nonfiction books.